Kids' Travel Guide

Los Angeles

FlyingKids Presents:

KIDS' TRAVEL GUIDE
LOS ANGELES

Author: Kelsey Fox, Shiela H. Leon

Editor: Carma Graber

Designer: Slavisa Zivkovic

Cover design: Francesca Guido

Illustrations: Slavisa Zivkovic, Francesca Guido

Published by FlyingKids Limited

Visit us @ www.theflyingkids.com

Contact us: leonardo@theflyingkids.com

ISBN 978-1-910994-33-7

TABLE OF CONTENTS

This is the only page for parents in this book ...

Dear Parents,

If you bought this book, you're probably planning a family trip with your kids. You are spending a lot of time and money in the hopes that this family vacation will be pleasant and fun. Of course, you would like your children to get to know the city you are visiting—a little of its geography, local history, important sites, culture, customs, and more. And you hope they will always remember the trip as a very special experience.

The reality is often quite different. Parents find themselves frustrated as they struggle to convince their kids to join a tour or visit a landmark, while the kids just want to stay in and watch TV. Or the kids are glued to their mobile devices and don't pay much attention to the new sights and places of interest. Many parents are disappointed when they return home and discover that their kids don't remember much about the trip and the new things they learned.

That's exactly why the Kids' Travel Guide series was created. With the Kids' Travel Guides, young children become researchers and active participants in the trip. During the vacation, kids will read relevant facts about the city you are visiting. The Kids' Travel Guides include puzzles, tasks to complete, useful tips, and other recommendations along the way.

The kids will meet Leonardo—their tour guide. Leonardo encourages them to experiment, explore, and be more involved in the family's activities—as well as to learn new information and make memories throughout the trip. In addition, kids are encouraged to document and write about their experiences during the trip, so that when you return home, they will have a memoir that will be fun to look at and reread again and again. The Kids' Travel Guides support children as they get ready for the trip, visit new places, learn new things, and finally, return home.

The *Kids' Travel Guide — Los Angeles* focuses on the City of Angels. In it, children will find background information on Los Angeles and its special attractions. The *Kids' Travel Guide — Los Angeles* concentrates on central sites that are recommended for children. At each of these sites, interesting facts, action items, and quizzes await your kids. You, the parents, are invited to participate or to find an available bench and relax while you enjoy your active children.

If you are traveling to Los Angeles, you may also want to get the *Kids' Travel Guide — USA*. It focuses on the country of the United States—its geography, history, unique culture, traditions, and more—using the fun and interesting style of the Kids' Travel Guide series.

Have a great Family Trip!

Hi, Kids!

If you are reading this book, it means you are llucky—you are going to Los Angeles!

You may have noticed that your parents are getting ready for the journey. They have bought travel guides, looked for information on the Internet, and printed pages of information. They are talking to friends and people who have already visited Los Angeles, in order to learn about it and know what to do, where to go, and when … But this is not just another guidebook for your parents.

This book is for you only—the young traVeler.

So what is this book all about?

First and foremost, meet Leonardo, your very own personal guide on this trip. Leonardo has visited many places around the world.
(Guess how he got there?) He will be with you throughout the book and the trip. Leonardo will tell you all about the places you will visit … It is always good to learn a little about the city you are visiting and its history beforehand. Leonardo will give you many ideas, quizzes, tips, and other surprises. He will accompany you while you are packing and leaving home. He will stay in the hotel with you (don't worry—it doesn't cost more money)! And he will see the sights with you until you return home.

A travel diary - the beginning!
Going to Los Angeles!!!

How did you get to Los Angeles?

By plane / train / car / other

Date of arrival _Aug, 13, 2017_ Time _____

Date of departure _Aug, 19, 2017_

All in all, we will stay in Los Angeles for __6__ days.

Is this your first visit? (YES) NO

Where will you sleep?

(In a hotel) / in a campsite / in an apartment / other

What places are you planning to visit?

Dodger Staidnm, unversal,
Disney land, Hollywood, Nickeloredens
Studios, Resteront / Hollywood blvd

What special activities are you planning to do?

_____

_____

_____

Are you excited about the trip?

This is an excitement indicator. Ask your family members how excited they are (from "not at all" up to "very, very much"), and mark each of their answers on the indicator. Leonardo has already marked the level of his excitement ...

very, very much

not at all   Leonardo

very mom
very

Who is traveling?

Write down the names of the family members traveling with you and their answers to the questions.

Name: Owen Bory

Age: 10

Has he or she visited Los Angeles **before?** yes / (no)

WHAT IS THE MOST EXCITING THING ABOUT YOUR UPCOMING TRIP?

evo-thing !.!!!!

Name: Olivia Bory

Age: 5

Has he or she visited Los Angeles **before?** yes / (no)

WHAT IS THE MOST EXCITING THING ABOUT YOUR UPCOMING TRIP?

exc,ed, going to the house

Name: Melissa BOry

Age: 38

Has he or she visited Los Angeles **before?** yes / (no)

WHAT IS THE MOST EXCITING THING ABOUT YOUR UPCOMING TRIP?

to be with family

Name: Matt bory

Age: 45

Has he or she visited Los Angeles **before?** yes / no

WHAT IS THE MOST EXCITING THING ABOUT YOUR UPCOMING TRIP?

Name:

Age:

Has he or she visited Los Angeles **before?** yes / no

WHAT IS THE MOST EXCITING THING ABOUT YOUR UPCOMING TRIP?

Preparations at home – do not forget …!

Mom or Dad will take care of packing clothes (how many pairs of pants, which comb to take …). So Leonardo will only tell you about the stuff he thinks you may want to bring along to Los Angeles.

Here's the Packing List Leonardo made for you. You can check off each item as you pack it:

☆ Kids' Travel Guide — Los Angeles—of course!

☆ Comfortable walking shoes

☆ A raincoat (One that folds up is best—sometimes it rains without warning …)

☆ A hat (and sunglasses, if you want)

☆ Pens and pencils

☆ Crayons and markers (It is always nice to color and paint.)

☆ A notebook or writing pad (You can use it for games or writing, or to draw or doodle in when you're bored …)

☆ A book to read

☆ Your smartphone/tablet or camera

☆ _____ Phone _____

☆ _____

Pack your things in a small bag (or backpack). You may also want to take these things:

☆ Snacks, fruit, candy, and chewing gum. If you are flying, it can help a lot during takeoff and landing, when there's pressure in your ears.

☆ Some games you can play while sitting down: electronic games, booklets of crossword puzzles, connect-the-numbers, etc.

Now let's see if you can find 12 items you should take on a trip in this word search puzzle:

- ☑ Leonardo
- ☑ walking shoes
- ☑ hat
- ☑ raincoat
- ☑ crayons
- ☑ book
- ☑ pencil
- ☑ camera
- ☑ snacks
- ☑ fruit
- ☑ patience
- ☑ good mood

P	A	T	I	E	N	C	E	A	W	F	G
A	L	R	T	S	G	Y	J	W	A	T	O
E	E	Y	U	Y	K	Z	K	M	L	W	O
Q	O	S	N	A	S	N	Y	S	K	G	D
H	N	R	Z	C	P	E	N	C	I	L	M
A	C	A	M	E	R	A	A	W	G	N	E	O
R	R	A	I	N	C	O	A	T	G	Q	O
Y	D	S	G	I	R	K	Z	K	S	H	D
S	O	A	C	O	A	E	T	K	H	A	T
F	R	U	I	T	Y	Q	O	V	O	D	A
B	O	O	K	F	O	H	Z	K	E	R	T
T	K	Z	K	A	N	S	I	E	S	Y	U
O	V	I	E	S	S	N	A	C	K	S	P

Los Angeles, California:
The City of Angels

Los Angeles is a big city in the state of California. California sits on the western coast of the United States of America. It borders the states of Oregon, Nevada, and Arizona and the country of Mexico—but most of California is coastline that touches the Pacific Ocean.

In terms of size, California is only the third largest state. But it has more people than any other state in America!

Help Leonardo find California on the map of the United States.

Can you also help him find how many neighboring states California has? _____

Quizzes!

Which two states are bigger than California? Use the map as a clue!

Every state in the United States has a nickname.
California's nickname is "The Golden State."
Can you think why California has this nickname? If you don't already know, you'll find the answer somewhere in this book ...

Does your state or country have a nickname? What is it? _The big apple_

A few more things about California:

The Capital: Sacramento
What is the capital of your state or country? _New York_

State Motto: "Eureka!" meaning "I have found It!"
(Do you know **what they found?** (G _ _ _ 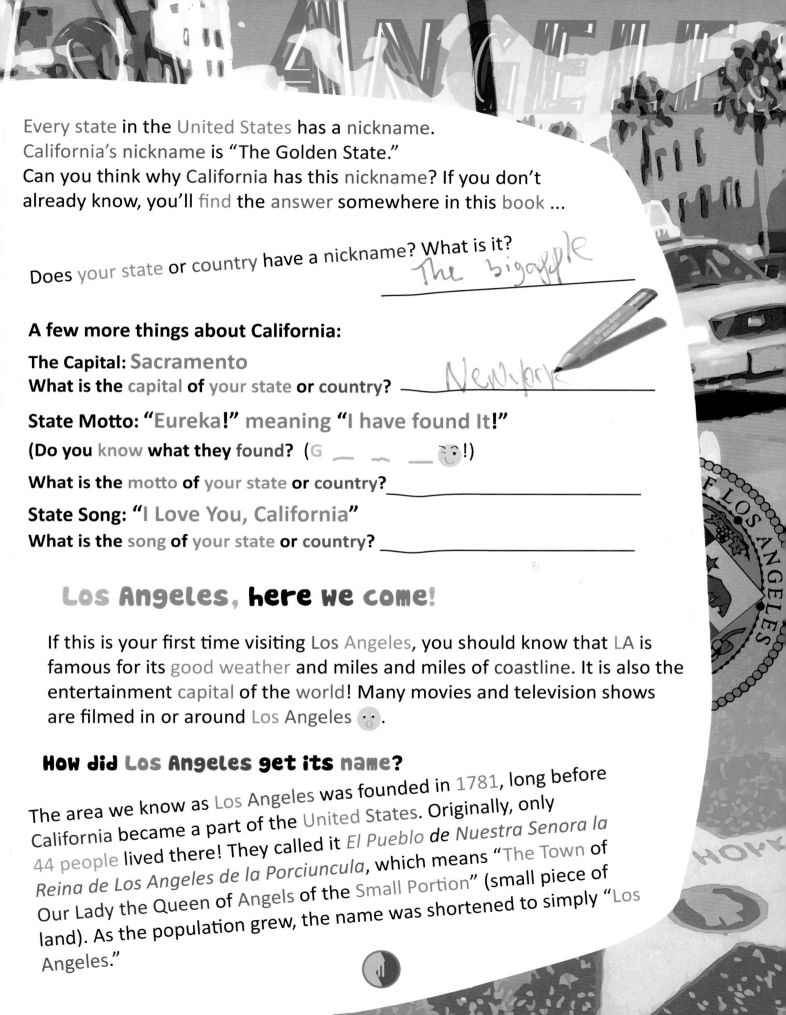 !)

What is the motto of your state or country? _____

State Song: "I Love You, California"
What is the song of your state or country? _____

Los Angeles, here we come!

If this is your first time visiting Los Angeles, you should know that LA is famous for its good weather and miles and miles of coastline. It is also the entertainment capital of the world! Many movies and television shows are filmed in or around Los Angeles.

How did Los Angeles get its name?

The area we know as Los Angeles was founded in 1781, long before California became a part of the United States. Originally, only 44 people lived there! They called it *El Pueblo de Nuestra Senora la Reina de Los Angeles de la Porciuncula*, which means "The Town of Our Lady the Queen of Angels of the Small Portion" (small piece of land). As the population grew, the name was shortened to simply "Los Angeles."

What does Los Angeles look like?

When we say "Los Angeles," we really mean the 88 cities that make up the greater Los Angeles area. If you look at the map below, you will see that Los Angeles is divided into five smaller areas called "counties":
Los Angeles, Riverside, Ventura, Orange, and San Bernardino.

Ventura
Los Angeles
San Bernardino
Griffith Observatory
Santa Monica Pier
Disneyland
Orange
Riverside
Long Beach Aquarium

Did you know?

Los Angeles has many nicknames. It can also be known as "LA," "City of Angels," "Southland," and "Lalaland." Can you think why Los Angeles is called each of these different nicknames?

In which county are you staying? Mark it on the map!

In which counties are these sites located?

Disneyland ————

Santa Monica Pier ————

Griffith Observatory ————

Long Beach Aquarium ————

ANSWERS

Disneyland—Orange County; Santa Monica Pier—LA County; Griffith Observatory—LA County; Long Beach Aquarium—LA County

The birth of Los Angeles

People have lived in the area that is now Los Angeles since 8000 BC. But it did not become a real city until the Spanish discovered it in the 1700s. "California" became part of the Spanish empire, and 44 people were sent to found and live in the new town that would become Los Angeles.

There were still many Native Americans living in Los Angeles and the rest of California, so the Spanish priests built 21 missions in an attempt to convert the natives to Christianity. These missions are still standing, and they are great places to visit!

When Mexico won its independence from Spain, the population of Los Angeles nearly tripled! People came from America, Europe, and other parts of Mexico to live in this beautiful area.

In May 1846, the Mexican-American War broke out. After two years of fighting, the war ended, and California officially became a part of the United States. However, Mexican culture is still very important to Los Angeles.

Did you know?

During your visit to Los Angeles, you will see many cities and street signs with Spanish and Mexican names. You will also see a lot of houses and buildings that have been built in the Spanish style! Now you know why!

Things you'll see only in Los Angeles

Movie sets and studios, sandy beaches, and glamorous people and houses—there are plenty of attractions in Los Angeles for you to choose from 😯.
Now it's time for Leonardo to lend a hand! He has gathered information about the most recommended sights and activities.

MOVIE SETS

Los Angeles is the home of the entertainment business. Most movies and television shows are filmed right here in LA, so always keep your eyes open for filming sites. When you see a bunch of white trailers, a lot of people, and movie cameras, you will know that you have stumbled upon a film set.

TRAFFIC

Unfortunately, Los Angeles is also known for its traffic 😣. As your family drives around, you will likely notice the packs of cars on streets and freeways. But don't let this frustrate you! Once you know that traffic is a normal part of Los Angeles culture, you can make it fun. Play a fun game like:

● The ABC Game
Go through the alphabet using street and building signs. For example, you can start with "A" and say "Angeles" if you see a sign that says "Los Angeles." The next person in the car would then find a sign that begins with the letter "B."

● The License Plate Game
Each car has a license plate that tells which state it's from. Find cars from different states and mark the states off of a list. We spotted cars from _____ different states.

The Hollywood Sign

The Hollywood Sign is one of the most famous symbols of Los Angeles. You have probably seen it many times in books, magazines, movies, and television shows.

Did you know?

The Hollywood Sign has been there for almost 100 years! Originally, it said "Hollywoodland," but the letters began to fall apart from neglect. Many famous residents of Los Angeles stepped in to help save the famous letters. Today, the sign just says "Hollywood." It is now a permanent and well-cared-for part of Los Angeles.

Visitors aren't allowed to get close to the Hollywood Sign, but you will have many opportunities to see it! Since the sign sits high up in the Hollywood Hills, it can be seen from many different places throughout Los Angeles.

 Tip!

Throughout this book, Leonardo has left tips on where and how to get a great view of the Hollywood Sign. You can follow his tips and find some of your own! Write down the different places where you can see the Hollywood Sign. Are these views good or bad?

This view is ...

	Good	Okay	Not so good
Hollywood sign			
Food			
City dodges stadium			
Calfionia			

100%

The Hollywood Walk of Fame

One of Hollywood's most famous sightseeing attractions is a sidewalk! But the Walk of Fame isn't just any sidewalk—it's lined with fancy pink stars with the names of the world's most famous people in entertainment. Spend a few minutes walking along the Walk of Fame and see if you can spot stars that have the names of any of your favorite movie and TV stars!

How to get a star on the Walk of Fame

If entertainers want to have their very own star, they must first be very famous. After all, these stars will be there forever. Second, they must be nominated. Then if they are chosen, they must pay $30,000 !

All along the Walk of Fame, celebrity impersonators and characters take pictures with fans. You might see famous characters like SpongeBob, Darth Vader, Marilyn Monroe, or others. Write down which characters you see:

_____

_____

_____

_____

Did you know?

You will notice different symbols beneath the names in the stars. The symbols are a movie camera, a radio microphone, a television, theater masks, and a record album. Can you think what each of these symbols says about the famous person?

Did you know?

There are currently more than 2,800 stars on the Hollywood Walk of Fame! Every month, one or two more people get their stars. That's a lot of stars!

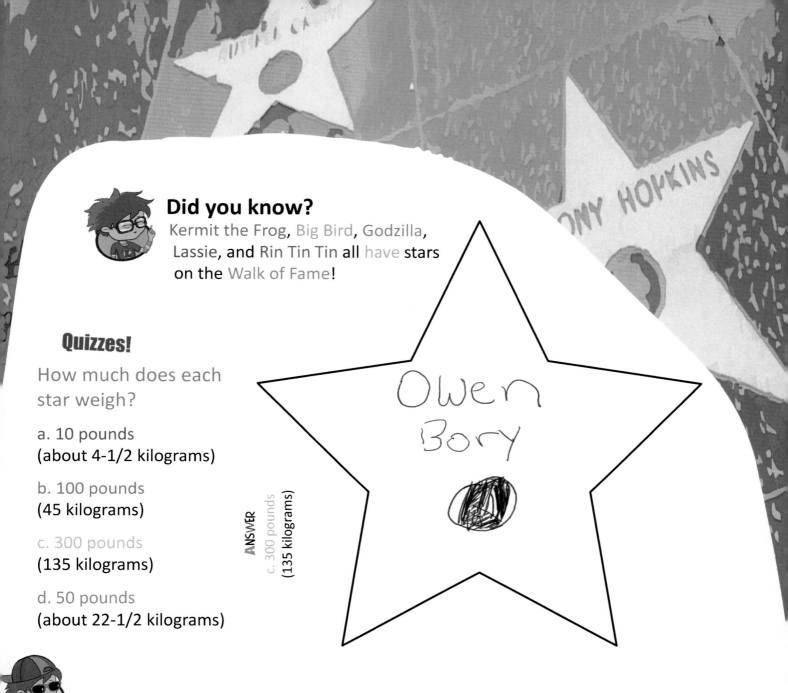

Did you know?
Kermit the Frog, Big Bird, Godzilla, Lassie, and Rin Tin Tin all have stars on the Walk of Fame!

Quizzes!

How much does each star weigh?

a. 10 pounds
(about 4-1/2 kilograms)

b. 100 pounds
(45 kilograms)

c. 300 pounds
(135 kilograms)

d. 50 pounds
(about 22-1/2 kilograms)

ANSWER
c. 300 pounds
(135 kilograms)

Owen
Bory

Design the star above to look like one on the Walk of Fame. You can copy one that you see, or make one for yourself!

What name is on your star?

Owen Bory

What symbol is on your star?

Hollywood Boulevard

As you already know, the Walk of Fame is on Hollywood Boulevard—where you'll also see many old and famous hotels. But do you notice something else Hollywood Boulevard has a lot of?

Hollywood Boulevard is home to three of the world's most famous theaters: the Chinese Theater, El Capitan, and the Dolby Theater. As you walk down Hollywood Boulevard, you can spend some time visiting each of them.

CHINESE THEATER

This theater—most commonly known as Grauman's Chinese Theater—is one of the most well-known theaters in the world. It was built all the way back in the 1920s. Since then, the Chinese Theater has hosted many movie premieres, including the Disney movies *The Jungle Book* and *Mary Poppins*. But the theater is most famous for its cement! If you look around, you will see that many famous movie stars have left their handprints and names in the cement in the theater courtyard! Do you see any people you know?

Some movie stars have left more than just their handprints. For example, Whoopi Goldberg left an imprint of one of her dreadlocks to honor her famous hairstyle. Can you find which movie stars left the following extras?

"You made my day." _____

A hoofprint (Hint: There are three to choose from.) _____

An imprint of her "million-dollar leg" _____

ANSWERS

Clint Eastwood; Famous horse stars Tony, Trigger, and Champion; Betty Grable, a movie star in the 1940s and '50s.

Disney's El Capitan Theater

Across the street from the Chinese Theater is Disney's El Capitan ("The Captain") Theater. Movie theaters used to be called "movie palaces," and El Capitan is one of the few theaters left in the world that we still call a "palace." Can you tell why?

El Capitan is a great place to see a movie! The theater only plays Disney movies. Along with each movie there's either a performance by a live character, a prop exhibit, or an interactive game!

Did you know?

A "premiere" is when the actors and filmmakers of a movie or television show get to watch the result of all their hard work for the very first time. It is usually a big party! Almost all of Disney's movies and television shows have their premieres at El Capitan Theater. If you are lucky, you will see a movie premiere when you visit El Capitan!

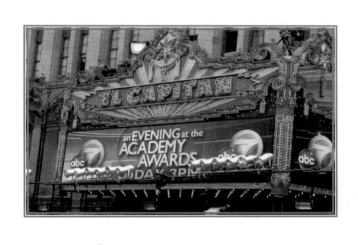

Which Disney movie was playing at El Capitan during your visit?

_____

_____

Did you stay to watch the movie?

_____

What fun things did you see at El Capitan?

_____

_____

Tip!

Attached to the theater is an old-fashioned soda fountain. You can get a tasty ice cream treat that has the same theme as the Disney movie playing at the theater!

The Dolby Theater

The Dolby Theater is famous because it is the home of the Academy Awards ceremony called "The Oscars." Every year, Hollywood's most famous actors, actresses, and filmmakers celebrate the best movies of the year. The movies and stars that are voted the very best in their categories win a statue nicknamed the "Oscar." People all over the world watch the Oscars that take place right here at this theater.

Tip!

As long as you aren't visiting LA during the Oscars, you can take a tour of the Dolby Center. You will see the beautiful theater, learn all about the Oscars, and even see a real Oscar!

Tip!

Remember our search for the Hollywood Sign? Walk to the far back patio of the Highland Center—the mall that's attached to the Dolby Theater. This is considered the very best view of the Hollywood Sign. What do you think?

Did you know?

More than 700 million people around the world watch the Oscars. Do you watch it from your home?

Sometimes movie stars sign autographs for their fans.

Leonardo wrote his autograph.

Leonardo

What does your autograph look like?

Tour a movie studio

You are probably learning a lot about movies and television on your trip to Los Angeles, but did you know you can visit an actual movie studio? There are many studios you can visit. Some of the famous ones are Warner Brothers Studios, Universal Studios, and Paramount Studios.

Which studio(s) did you visit? _Nickloden, dodger, everything_

A movie studio treasure hunt

There are a lot of things to see on your studio tour! Which of these things did you see? (Remember, if you need help, look over the vocabulary list on the next page.)

▢ "Props" and costumes

What genre of movie do you think these belong to? _____

▮ A "green light"

▯ A "set"

What did it look like? _____

▮ A "facade"

▮ A movie star! _____

What was he/she doing? _____

21

Learn to speak movie!

Here are some common filmmaking terms that will help you get the most out of your studio tour.

"RED LIGHT"

On each studio, you will see a number and a light. If the light is red, it means that a movie or television show is filming, and visitors are not allowed to enter or open the door.

How many red lights did you see? _____

What do you think a "green light" means? _____

"PROPS"

Props are the different objects used in a movie or television show. For example, if a scene takes place in a café, some props might include a cup of coffee, the book the actor is reading, and a plate with a snack on it.

"GENRE"

The genre describes what kind of movie it is: comedy, drama, mystery, thriller, or romantic comedy, to name a few.

"FACADE"

A facade is a set that is made to look like a building, but is actually only the front.

Make a movie about a moment in your life using your phone or camera.

What genre is it? _____

What does the set look like? _____

What kinds of props are on the set? _____

California Science Center

The California Science Center is popular with both visitors and people who live in LA. The museum was opened in 1998 in downtown Los Angeles. It has four major exhibit areas—plus some fun temporary exhibits that everyone in your family will be able to enjoy.

Whether you are spending a day at the museum or only a few hours, Leonardo has found the must-see highlights in each exhibit area. Mark which attractions you see, and then add your own favorites!

WORLD OF LIFE—Learn about all of the things that make up human life, from the single-celled bacteria to the trillions of cells in your human body.

☐ Energy Factory

☐ BodyWorks

☐ The Cell Lab

☐ _____

ECOSYSTEMS—Learn about all the plants, animals, people, weather, water, and soil that make up our environment.

CREATIVE WORLD—Explore the benefits and consequences of inventions and innovation.

☐ Earthquake Experience

☐ Auto Design Decisions

☐ _____

☐ Bobcat Tilt Table

☐ Kelp Forest

☐ Underwater Island Life

☐ _____

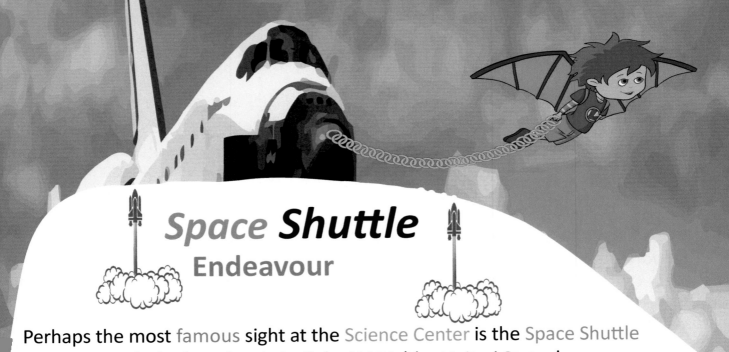

Space **Shuttle**
Endeavour

Perhaps the most famous sight at the Science Center is the Space Shuttle Endeavour. It's the last shuttle built by NASA (the United States' space agency). The Endeavour took its first flight in May 1992. It continued to fly for 19 years, and was finally retired in 2012. Now it's a permanent exhibit here at the Science Center for visitors and Los Angeles residents to admire and ENJOY!

Quizzes!

In its 19-year career, Endeavour made _____ trips around the Earth.

a. 1,000

b. 4,600

c. 10,600

d. 2,600

ANSWER
b. 4,600

Tip!

The California Story exhibit includes the Waste Collection System (um ... toilet 😊) from the Endeavour. Take a few minutes to learn about the tricky task of going to the bathroom when there is no gravity to help out!

California **Science** Center **summary**

My favorite exhibit: _____

Most interesting exhibit: _____

Most boring exhibit: _____

Strangest exhibit: _____

An interesting fact I learned: _____

_____

Beverly Hills

In the early years of movies, the very first movie stars built their homes in a small town called Beverly Hills. Over the years, many other people joined them, and today, Beverly Hills is one of the most famous cities in the world. Though it is not a very big town, Beverly Hills is known for its beautiful people, big mansions, fancy restaurants, and exclusive shopping. People who live in Beverly Hills include actors and filmmakers, famous authors and journalists, successful business people, and even royalty!

Did you know?
Every street in Beverly Hills is lined with trees, but no two streets have the same kind of trees.

True or False?
Beverly Hills is the only city in the world that has no hospital, no cemetery, no billboards, and no phone or power wires.

ANSWER
True

Tip!
Wilshire Boulevard in Beverly Hills is the perfect place to have lunch while people-watching.

Did you know?
Horses have been banned in Beverly Hills since 1930.

Rodeo Drive

Rodeo Drive (pronounced Ro-DAY-oh) is a street in Beverly Hills that is lined with glamorous and expensive shops and boutiques. Everything in these stores is very expensive, but even if you're not buying anything, it is fun to look and "window shop ."

Tip!

If you look closely, you will spot black curtains on the windows of some of the stores and boutiques. Most of the time, these windows are open so people can see inside the store. But if the curtains are closed, it means a famous person is shopping in the store! The curtains keep photographers from taking pictures through the windows. Be on the lookout !

Find Two Rodeo Drive and stand near the famous Rodeo Drive sign at the beginning of the street (if you need help, look at the picture). Face away from the busy street (Dayton Way).

What is in front of you? _____

ANSWER
cobblestone streets and fancy boutiques

What is behind you? _____

ANSWER
Dayton Way, Seafood Grille, Harry Winston

What is to your right? _____

ANSWER
Rodeo Drive, Louis Vuitton

Did you know?

House of Bijan, the most expensive store in the world, is on Rodeo Drive. If you want to shop there, you must first make a reservation! If you find House of Bijan, look on the front window. Engraved there are the names of some of House of Bijan's famous customers.

What is to your left? _____

ANSWER
Dayton Way, shops

Griffith Observatory

Not only is Griffith Observatory one of the most popular attractions in Los Angeles, it is also one of the most important centers for astronomy (the study of space) in the world!

Tip! Walk along the railing on the right side of the Observatory parking lot to see a great view of the Hollywood Sign!

What to do at the Observatory!
The Griffith Observatory is not a very big museum, but it has a lot to do!
Here are Leonardo's "must-see" attractions!

☐ Visit the Planetarium and learn all about stars and planets.

☐ Use a telescope to explore the map of the universe. (It's the largest telescope of its kind in the entire world.)

☐ Stick around when they turn off the lights, and learn about the night sky and how it changes when we are sleeping.

Quizzes!

Help Leonardo count! How many planets are in our solar system?

Write the name of each planet.

_____

_____

_____

_____

_____

_____

_____

ANSWERS

Eight planets: Mercury, Venus, Earth, Mars, Jupiter, Saturn, Uranus, and Neptune

Tip!

Find **one of the** Observatory's **many** terraces **and look out over the** whole city. **This will give you a** good idea **of just how big Los Angeles is. This is also a great spot for a** family picture**!**

Which **of these** astronomers discovered **the law of** gravity?

_____

Find **the** Astronomers Monument **near the entrance to the** Observatory. **The monument** lists the names **of six of the greatest astronomers of all time. Find the** six names **in the word search below!**

Hipparchus

Copernicus

Galileo

Kepler

Newton

Herschel

```
H N O T W E N V U Z
I Y L E R E L P E K
P J T S R R C I R C
P S L E H C S R E H
A G A L I L E O S C
R R R N C Y L K Y J
C O P E R N I C U S
H T T C O A R C M M
U S P T B B R V L U
S Z Z A N N P W D C
```

Take a hike!

The Observatory is only one of the fun things to do on your visit! Near the parking lot is the entrance to the Mount Hollywood Hiking Trail. This easy trail is a fun way to see amazing views of Los Angeles and the Hollywood Hills—and up-close views of the Hollywood Sign.

Santa Monica Pier

The Santa Monica Pier is an amusement park and beach near the ocean in Santa Monica. This is a fun place to spend some time playing games, going on rides, and eating yummy food like the famous "hot dog on a stick." The nearby beach is perfect for spending the rest of the day swimming in the Pacific Ocean, playing in the sand, or taking a catnap.

Did you know?
Titanic, Iron Man, and Hannah Montana: The Movie all have scenes that were filmed at the Santa Monica Pier. Can you think of any other movies with scenes from the Pier?

Rides!
The Santa Monica Pier is famous for its amusement park rides, like the West Coaster roller coaster, the Ferris wheel, the bumper cars, a drop tower, and lots of others.

My favorite ride: _____

The scariest ride: _____

Foods I ate: _____

My favorite street performer: _____

Did you know?
The Pier hasn't always been tons of fun. When it first opened in 1909, its purpose was to carry sewage out past the breakers (the place where waves break). This lasted only seven years though, because the beach and pier quickly became popular spots to hang out.

La Brea Tar Pits

Can you imagine the big, modern city of Los Angeles as a prehistoric valley with thousands of plants and animals? Until about 11,000 years ago, Los Angeles was filled with wildlife! At the spot where the Page Museum now stands, there were large pools

of "tar," a black, sticky, oil-like substance. Many animals got stuck in these "tar pits," where they died and remained for thousands of years until paleontologists (scientists who study fossils) began to find them.

More than one million fossils from 650 different species have been found in the La Brea Tar Pits.

Did you know?

Remember *El Pueblo de Nuestra Senora la Reina de Los Angeles de la Porciuncula*, the small town from which Los Angeles was founded? The citizens of that village used the tar and asphalt from the tar pits as fuel and to waterproof everything from baskets to the roofs of their houses.

What is the most common large animal found in the tar pits?

a. Mastodon

b. Dire wolf

Quizzes!

c. Camel

d. Dinosaur

ANSWER

b. Dire wolf. More than 4,000 dire wolves have been found. Most of them probably became trapped in the tar while they were trying to catch and eat other trapped animals.

We know which animals lived a long time ago because scientists find fossils (bones). Fossils can tell us what an animal ate and how it moved, died, and more. Most importantly, fossils tell us what the animal looked like.

As you learn about different prehistoric animals, match the prehistoric animal to its modern-day relative:

Dire wolf   Tree sloth

Yesterday's camel Elephant

Ground sloth   Mountain lion

Saber-toothed cat Coyote

Mastodon   Llama

Do you remember what "paleontology" is?

ANSWER

The study of fossils.

My favorite prehistoric animal is the ——————— .

It lived during the ——————. My animal is ——— in size compared to other animals of its time. Its teeth are ——————, which tells me that it ate ——————— . It walked on ——— legs. My animal looks like it moved —————, because ————————————— . A living animal similar to my animal is the

——————————— .

Aquarium of the Pacific

By now, you have probably seen the ocean and maybe even spent some time playing in the sand at the beach. When you visit the Aquarium of the Pacific in Long Beach, you can learn about what goes on underneath those beautiful blue-green waters.

Did You Know?

Long Beach is a popular coastal city near Los Angeles. It's known for its university, its "laid-back vibe" (American slang for "relaxed feeling"), the *Queen Mary* ship, and of course, its aquarium. If you are going on a cruise, your ship is likely to leave from the Port of Long Beach.

The Aquarium of the Pacific has more than 11,000 ocean animals in 32 exhibits! All of the exhibits are especially designed to teach you about the waters of the Pacific Ocean.

Look at the map below.

How many oceans can you count? __*J2*__

Which one is the biggest? __*Atlantic Pacific*__

Which one is closest to where you live? __*calliWA*__

ANSWERS

There are five oceans: Pacific, Atlantic, Indian, Arctic, and Southern. The Pacific Ocean is the biggest. It covers more than 30 percent of the earth!

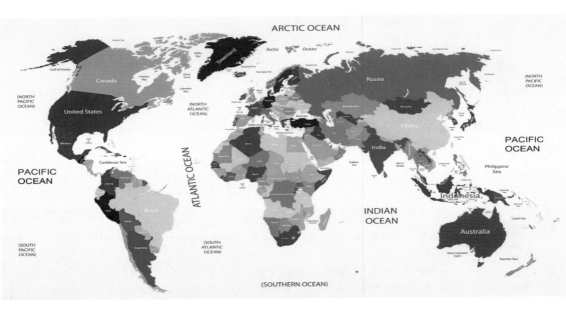

There are many great exhibits at the Aquarium of the Pacific. Which ones did you see?

- ☐ Ocean Exploration
- ☐ June Keyes Penguin Habitat
- ☐ Whales: Voices in the Sea
- ☐ Molina Animal Care Center
- ☐ Shark Lagoon
- ☐ Lorikeet Forest
- ☐ Aquarium Webcams

Did you know?

There are more than 360 different species of sharks in the oceans. They come in all different shapes and sizes. The tiny pygmy shark is less than 1 foot (about 1/3 meter) in length, while the big whale shark can grow to 50 feet (15-1/4 meters)!

Tip! If you really enjoyed the La Brea Tar Pits and want to learn more about prehistoric animals, spend a few minutes watching *Monsters of the Deep* at the Aquarium. This 4D film will take you back to millions of years ago when some pretty interesting animals lived in the ocean.

Did you know?
Experts estimate that 99 percent of the earth's oceans are still unexplored. That's a lot of ocean!

Now that you are an expert on oceans and ocean animals 😊, help Leonardo solve the riddle by filling in the sentences with words from the word bank.

WORD BANK

Adaptation	Echolocation	Omnivore	Algae	Mammal
Baleen	Habitat	Predator	Camouflage	
Herbivore	Plankton	Food chain	Prey	
Carnivore	Invertebrate	Vertebrate	Cetaceans	

1. _ _ _ _ _ _ are hairy plates inside the mouth of a whale, used for filtering food from water.

2. An animal that eats other animals is called a _ _ _ _ _ _ _ _ _ .

3. Animals that eat only plants are called _ _ _ _ _ _ _ _ _ _ .

4. An animal without a spinal column is an _ _ _ _ _ _ _ _ _ _ _ _ .

5. An animal that is eaten by another animal is called _ _ _ _ .

6. _ _ _ _ _ _ _ _ are the places where animals live (their homes).

7. _ _ _ _ _ _ _ _ _ _ _ _ is a behavior, shape, color, or pattern that helps an animal blend into its surroundings.

8. A _ _ _ _ _ _ _ _ _ _ is when smaller organisms are eaten by larger organisms, which are in turn eaten by even larger organisms.

ANSWERS
1. Baleen; 2. Carnivore; 3. Herbivores; 4. Invertebrate; 5. Prey; 6. Habitats; 7. Camouflage; 8. Food Chain.

A Riddle!

Why did the shark spit out the clown?

_ _ _ _ _ _ _   _ _   _ _ _ _ _ _   _ _ _ _ _!

ANSWER

Because he tasted funny!

4

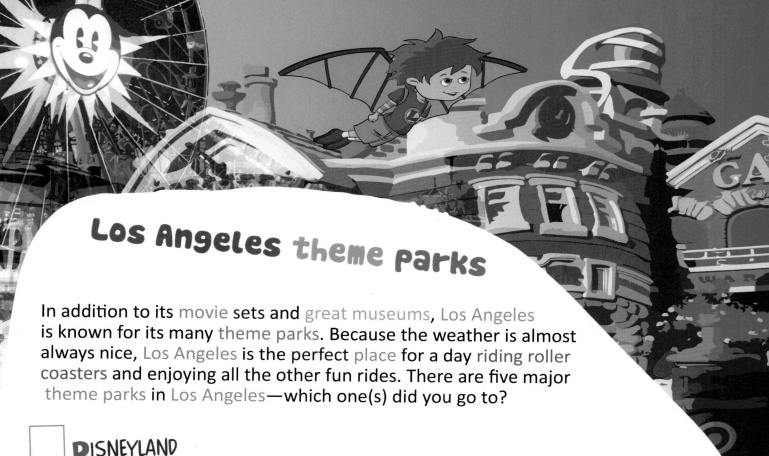

Los Angeles theme parks

In addition to its movie sets and great museums, Los Angeles is known for its many theme parks. Because the weather is almost always nice, Los Angeles is the perfect place for a day riding roller coasters and enjoying all the other fun rides. There are five major theme parks in Los Angeles—which one(s) did you go to?

☐ DISNEYLAND

It's called "The Happiest Place on Earth," and Disneyland has been entertaining children and families since 1955. Based on the magic and wonder of Disney movies, Disneyland is a great place to spend a day or two. Favorite rides include Pirates of the Caribbean, Space Mountain, Indiana Jones, Splash Mountain, and many more!

Did you know?

The popular ride Soarin' Over California will make you feel as if you are gliding over the whole state. You'll also smell different California smells like the ocean and citrus!

Quizzes! The creator of Mickey Mouse and Disneyland was a man named:

a. Walt Disney
b. Michael Eisner
c. Donald Duck
d. John Smith

☐ DISNEYLAND'S CALIFORNIA ADVENTURE

In 2000, Disneyland decided to add another park. The new park's theme is California, and it's a great place to have fun and learn all about the state you are visiting. The park has rides based on Yosemite, Hollywood, San Francisco, and the Santa Monica Pier—and even a CarsLand!

ANSWER
a. Walt Disney

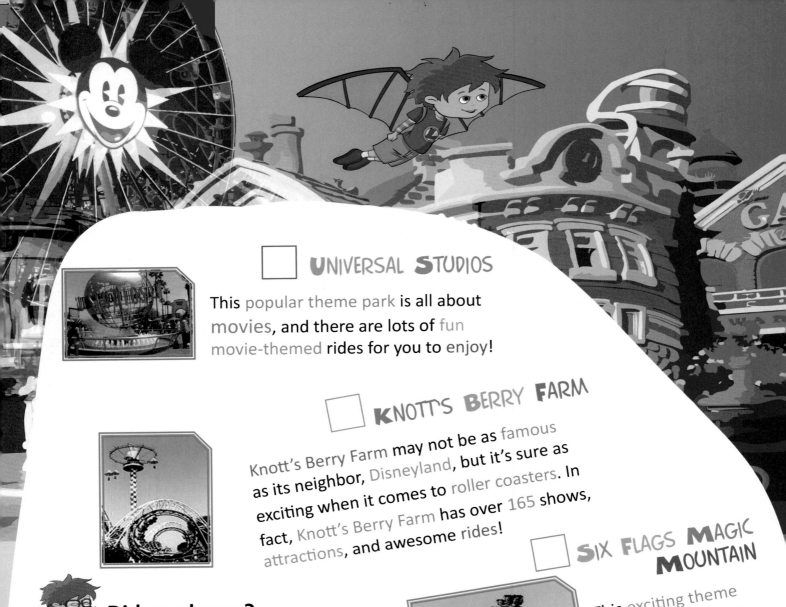

☐ **UNIVERSAL STUDIOS**

This popular theme park is all about movies, and there are lots of fun movie-themed rides for you to enjoy!

☐ **KNOTT'S BERRY FARM**

Knott's Berry Farm may not be as famous as its neighbor, Disneyland, but it's sure as exciting when it comes to roller coasters. In fact, Knott's Berry Farm has over 165 shows, attractions, and awesome rides!

☐ **SIX FLAGS MAGIC MOUNTAIN**

This exciting theme park has something for everyone in the family: fun roller coasters, a Bugs Bunny World playland, arcade games, stunt shows, parades, and more! On a really hot day, you can also head next door to Hurricane Harbor, a water park with pools, water slides, an African river, a tropical lagoon, and rafts.

Did you know?

Knott's Berry Farm was America's first theme park! In 1920, Walter Knott and his wife began selling pies to make extra money during the Great Depression. Soon they were selling almost 100 pies per day—so Walter opened up an Old West Ghost Town to entertain people while they waited in line for their pies. The rest is history!

Tip! On a hot Southern California day, the Jurassic Park ride at Knott's Berry Farm is a great way to cool down. A boat-car takes you through Jurassic Park, where you'll see dinosaurs that will try to splash you with water! Bring your towel!

Did you know?

Six Flags Magic Mountain has 18 world-class roller coasters—more than any other place in the world!

Quizzes!

Can you guess the famous Los Angeles attractions below?

1. I was once a real estate sign advertising the beautiful area known as Hollywoodland. But when people forgot about me, I started to fall apart. Thanks to some very special people, I was saved. I'm now one of the most recognizable sights in the whole world.

_____

(The Hollywood Sign)

2. During my 19-year career, I made almost 5,000 trips around the Earth! Now I'm enjoying my retirement at the California Science Center, where I'm on display to teach people of all ages about space. _____

(Space Shuttle Endeavour)

3. I am older than almost everything you have seen in Los Angeles. In fact, I am millions of years old. I have consumed thousands of animals, although I'm not a predator. Today, I'm the location for a popular museum—where paleontologists teach people about what Los Angeles was like back in my day. _____

(La Brea Tar Pits)

Trivia of Los Angeles

1. Which popular Los Angeles attraction was the very first theme park in the United States?
   a. Disneyland
   b. Knott's Berry Farm
   c. Universal Studios
   d. California Adventure

2. Every year, the Oscars are held at which famous theater?
   a. Dolby Theater
   b. El Capitan
   c. Chinese Theater
   d. ArcLight Cinemas

3. California officially became a state after which war?
   a. American Revolution
   b. American Civil War
   c. Mexican-American War
   d. 100 Years' War

ANSWERS

1.b, 2.a, 3.c

A Los Angeles crossword

ACROSS
3. Number of counties that make up Los Angeles
6. The study of fossils
7. The state in which you will find Los Angeles
9. "The City of _____"

DOWN
1. The Academy Awards ceremony
2. The famous roller coaster at the Santa Monica Pier
4. These are banned in Beverly Hills
5. The space agency that built the Space Shuttle Endeavour
8. Hollywood Walk of _____

Can you break the code?

Use the key below to decode Leonardo's journal entry about his trip to Los Angeles.

G = A   Z = O   B = E   J = I

I had a great time in LZS QNGBLBS (_ _ _ _ _ _ _ _ _ _)! I visited lots of museums and even went to a MZVJB STUDJZ (_ _ _ _ _ _ _ _ _ _ _)!

One of my favorite museums was La Brea Tar Pits, where I learned about prehistoric animals like the mammoth and DJRB WZLF (_ _ _ _ _ _ _ _). Los Angeles sure was interesting a million years ago! At the Santa Monica Pier, we saw lots of street performers, and I got to ride the CQRZUSBL (_ _ _ _ _ _ _ _).

My favorite thing in Los Angeles was the California Science Center with the SPQCB SHUTTLB BNDBQVZUR (_ _ _ _ _ _ _ _ _ _ _ _ _ _ _ _ _ _ _ _ _ _ _). Then again, I also loved the STQRS (_ _ _ _ _) on the Walk of Fame and the shopping on RZDBZ DRJVB (_ _ _ _ _ _ _ _ _ _). I guess I loved BVBRYTHJNG (_ _ _ _ _ _ _ _ _ _) about the beautiful City of Angels!

Unscramble the famous Los Angeles sites

Le Aaniptc Aerteth   _____   (El Capitan Theater)

Hdwlooylo Gnis   _____   (Hollywood Sign)

Voiem Utoids   _____   (Movie Studio)

SUMMARY OF THE TRIP

We had great fun—what a pity it is over ...

Which places did you visit? _____

_____

Whom did you meet ...

Did you meet tourists from other countries? **Yes / No**

If you did meet tourists, where did they come from?

(Name their nationalities): _____

Shopping and souvenirs ...

What did you buy on the trip? _____

What did you want to buy, but ended up not buying?

_____

Experiences

What are the most memorable experiences of the trip?

_____

_____

_____

_____

_____

_____

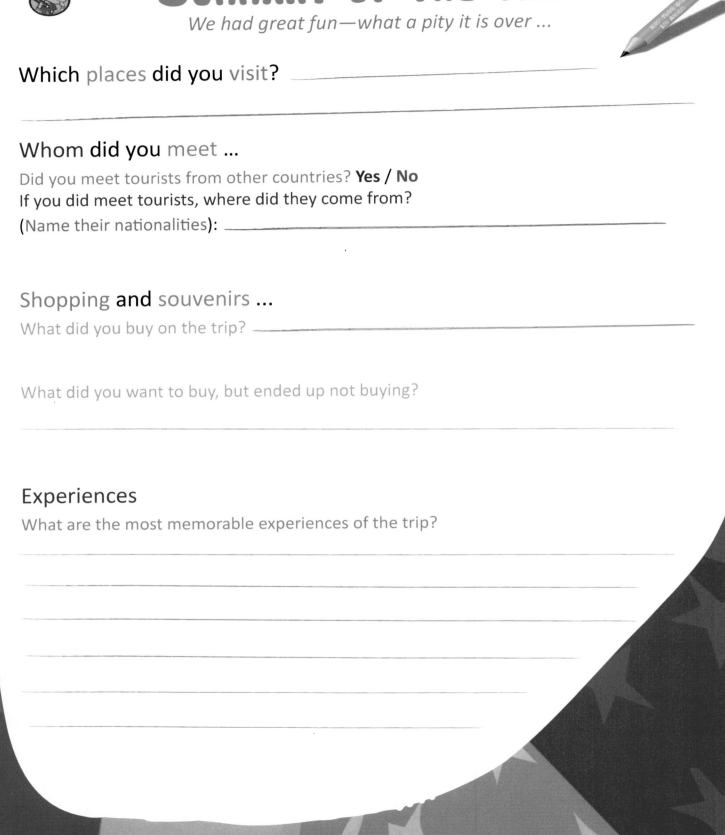

AND TO SUM IT ALL UP...

What were the most beautiful places and the best experiences of your journey?

First place –

Second place –

Third place –

And now,

a difficult tasks—talk with your family and decide:

What did everyone enjoy most on the trip?

Grand Prize –

A journal

Date	What **did we do?**

CITY OF LOS ANGELES

A journal

Date

What did we do?

_____   _____
_____   _____
_____   _____
_____   _____
_____   _____
_____   _____
_____   _____
_____   _____
_____   _____
_____   _____
_____   _____

Acknowledgment: All images except those mentioned below are from Shutterstock or public domain.
Attributions: 17m-By Elisa.rolle (Own work) [CC BY-SA 3.0 (http://creativecommons.org/licenses/by-sa/3.0)], via Wikimedia Commons; via Wikimedia Commons; 19m-By Greg in Hollywood (Greg Hernandez) (Flickr) [CC BY 2.0 (http://creativecommons.org/licenses/by/2.0)], via Wikimedia Commons; 20m-By Adam Fagen from Washington, DC, USA derivative work: Jullit31 (This file was derived from: Dolby Theatre.jpg:) [CC BY-SA 2.0 (http://creativecommons.org/licenses/by-sa/2.0)], via Wikimedia Commons; 23m-By Richard Kim (self-published from Wikipedia) [GFDL (http://www.gnu.org/copyleft/fdl.html) or CC BY 3.0 (http://creativecommons.org/licenses/by/3.0)], via Wikimedia Commons; 24m-By InSapphoWeTrust from Los Angeles, California, USA [CC BY-SA 2.0 (http://creativecommons.org/licenses/by-sa/2.0)], via Wikimedia Commons; 35mt-By Giovana Araujo Martins (Own work) [CC BY-SA 4.0 (http://creativecommons.org/licenses/by-sa/4.0)], via Wikimedia Commons; 36mc-By Orange County Archives [CC BY 2.0 (http://creativecommons.org/licenses/by/2.0)], via Wikimedia Commons.

Key: t=top;
b=bottom;
l=left;
r=right;
c=center;
m=main image;
bg=background

-3-

ENJOY MORE FUN ADVENTURES WITH LEONARDO

ITALY

THAILAND

FRANCE

USA

UNITED KINGDOM

SPECIAL EDITIONS

Get lots of information on travel—and the latest on new books and destinations—by checking out our website: www.theflyingkids.com

42185656R00027